E/Dor
5/2004
OKN

What's Inside a Police Car?

Sharon Gordon

BENCHMARK BOOKS

MARSHALL CAVENDISH
NEW YORK

Inside a Police Car

1. computer
2. engine
3. first-aid kit
4. flares

5 floodlight

6 handcuffs

7 radar gun

8 two-way radio

The police officers walk to their car. It is time to get to work!

The police car is built to help officers do their job.

It has a powerful *engine*. This makes it go faster than most cars.

Inside the police car, two officers can sit up front. A screen divides the front seat and backseat. This helps the officers stay safe.

The police car looks different from other cars. The name of the town is on the door. It has flashing lights on top.

The police car also has a loud *siren*.

The police officers are on their way to an emergency. The *computer* inside the police car shows them information about what happened.

The *dispatcher* gives them directions on the two-way radio.

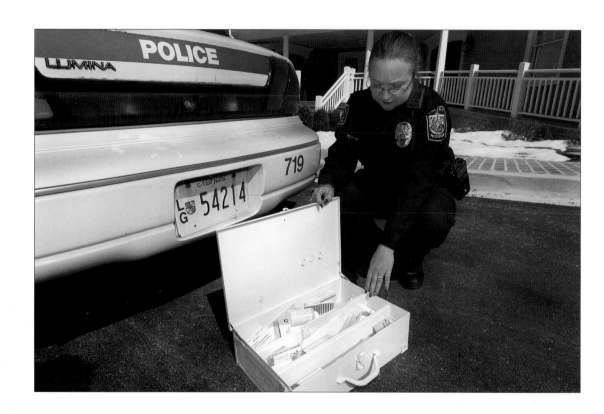

If someone is hurt, the police officers get the *first-aid kit* from the trunk. They may use an *oxygen tank* and mask to help someone breathe.

Sometimes the officers call for the ambulance.

The police car moves across town. An officer sets up the *radar gun* inside the police car. It can tell how fast other cars are going.

If a driver is speeding, the officer gives him a ticket.

18

The police officer arrives at a traffic jam. There has been an accident. She turns on the police car's flashing lights. She sets up *flares* to warn others.

Sometimes an officer speaks to people from inside the police car. She talks on a *loudspeaker*. She can tell drivers to pull over or turn back.

21

The dispatcher calls the police car on the two-way radio. Someone is reporting a lot of noise. There might be trouble.

The officers are ready for dangerous work. They have special tools for the job.

The police car has a *floodlight* to use at night. It lights up dark hiding places.

The police officers carry handcuffs. Handcuffs keep a person's hands close together. There is also a large gun inside the police car.

The officers are trained to use these tools safely.

But the officers will not need their tools tonight. They can keep them inside the police car.

Here is the troublemaker!

Challenge Words

computer—A machine that records, stores, and finds information.

dispatcher—A phone operator who takes emergency calls for the police, ambulance, and fire stations.

engine (en-juhn)—A machine that provides the power that moves a car.

first-aid kit—A box or bag that holds supplies to help a sick or injured person.

flares—Bright warning lights.

floodlight—A light on a police car that sends out a wide, bright ray of light.

loudspeaker—A tool that makes a person's voice loud enough to be heard in a large area.

oxygen tank (ak-si-juhn tank)—A tank that stores oxygen, a special gas that is needed to breathe.

radar gun—A tool that measures the speed of an object.

siren (sigh-run)—An electrical horn that makes a loud up-and-down warning sound.

Index

Page numbers in **boldface** are illustrations.

With thanks to Nanci Vargus, Ed.D.
and Beth Walker Gambro, reading consultants

ACKNOWLEDGMENTS
With thanks to the men and women of the Chevy Chase Village, Maryland,
Police Department and the Montgomery County, Maryland, Police Department

Benchmark Books
Marshall Cavendish
99 White Plains Road
Tarrytown, New York 10591-9001
www.marshallcavendish.com

Library of Congress Cataloging-in-Publication Data

Gordon, Sharon.
What's inside a police car? / by Sharon Gordon.
p. cm. — (Bookworms: What's inside?)
Includes index.
Summary: Describes how the equipment in a police car is used to help
people who are hurt, to monitor traffic, and to fight crime.
ISBN 0-7614-1565-3
1. Police vehicles—Juvenile literature. [1. Police vehicles. 2.
Police.] I. Title II. Series: Gordon, Sharon.   Bookworms. Just the opposite.

HV7936.V4G67 2003
363.2'32—dc21
2003006188

Photo Research by Anne Burns Images

Cover Photo by Jay Mallin

The photographs in this book are used with permission and through the courtesy of: *Jay Mallin*:
pp. 1, 2 (top right) (bottom), 3, 5, 6, 9, 10, 13, 14, 17, 18, 21, 25, 26, 28, 29.
Corbis: pp. 2 (top left), 12 DiMaggio/Kalish; p. 22 Tim Wright.

Series design by Becky Terhune

Printed in China
1   3   5   6   4   2